Henry Sebastian Bowden

Miniature life of Mary, virgin and mother

For every day of the month

Henry Sebastian Bowden

Miniature life of Mary, virgin and mother
For every day of the month

ISBN/EAN: 9783741142307

Manufactured in Europe, USA, Canada, Australia, Japa

Cover: Foto ©Andreas Hilbeck / pixelio.de

Manufactured and distributed by brebook publishing software (www.brebook.com)

Henry Sebastian Bowden

Miniature life of Mary, virgin and mother

MINIATURE
LIFE OF MARY,

VIRGIN AND MOTHER,

FOR

EVERY DAY OF THE MONTH.

COMPILED BY

HENRY SEBASTIAN BOWDEN,
OF THE ORATORY.

'Talis fuit Maria, ut ejus unius vita omnium sit disciplina.'
AMBROSE.

LONDON: BURNS AND OATES.
1880.

Imprimatur.

HENRICUS EDUARDUS,
Card. Archiep. Westmon.

TO THE

BROTHERS OF THE LITTLE ORATORY,

WHO,

BY THE FIRST RULE OF THEIR INSTITUTE,

TAKE

MARY

FOR

THEIR MOTHER AND ADVOCATE.

PREFACE.

IN deference to a wish repeatedly expressed by the readers of the *Miniature Lives of the Saints*, this little book has been drawn up on a similar model. The Life of Mary is divided into thirty-one days or sections, and is intended to supply spiritual reading on the mysteries of our B. Lady, for use throughout the year, as well as on her feasts, and during the month of Mary. It will also suggest thoughts for meditation on the Rosary and the Seven Dolours, and in many other devotions. The contents have been compiled and abbreviated from a variety of sources, among which may be specially mentioned the *Contemplations*, by J. Cross, O.S.F. (A.D. 1685).

The difficulty is undoubted of treating worthily a theme so exalted, and with so wide a range, as the life of Mary. The task, however, has been undertaken with some confidence, from the conviction that any words in our Lady's praise will meet with a response in Catholic hearts, and be welcomed for the sake of her, 'whom to think upon is perfect understanding.'

MEANS TO OBTAIN TRUE DEVOTION TO OUR LADY.

1. To make mental prayer on the mysteries of her life, and in her relationship to us.
2. To read books written in her praise, and to spread them among others, or to distribute her images or beads.
3. To recite her Little Office, Rosary, or any chaplets in her honour.
4. To invoke her daily at the Angelus, and by frequent ejaculations, but especially by the Hail Mary.
5. To wear one or more of her scapulars, or an image or medal of her.
6. To visit her altar, and to pay special reverence to her images.
7. To offer Mass or Communion in her honour, or to give alms for a Mass to be said for the same purpose.
8. To keep with great devotion her principal feasts, their novenas and octaves.
9. To gain indulgences for the soul in Purgatory most devoted to her in life.
10. To practise some mortification in her honour, especially on Saturday.
11. Above all, to imitate her virtues, without which true devotion to her is impossible.

PRACTICES IN HONOUR OF MARY.

The following practices may be drawn by lot, or otherwise chosen, at the beginning of a month.

1. Take a short time from your recreation to spend in solitude conversing with Mary.
2. Rise punctually in the morning, invoking the Morning Star.
3. Invoke her sixty-three times as 'Virgin Mother' in honour of her sixty-three years.
4. Visit in spirit one of her great sanctuaries.
5. Mortify your will three times as an offering to Mary.
6. Say three Glorias in honour of the saints and doctors who have explained and defended her prerogatives.
7. Kiss the book in which the name of Mary is written.
8. Ask Mary to be present with you during the day to drive away evil spirits.
9. Perform some act of kindness with inconvenience to yourself.
10. Say three Hail Marys in reparation for the blasphemies uttered against her.
11. Give an alms in honour of her poverty.
12. Invoke the saints who were related to her — SS. Joseph, Joachim, Anna, &c.
13. Mortify your sight, once or more, in honour of Mary's modesty.
14. Burn a candle before her image or picture.
15. Recall with devotion her words recorded

in the Gospel, remembering how many of your sins are committed in speech.

16. Say the Litany for the conversion of a soul for Mary to offer to God.

17. Shun idleness during the day in imitation of Mary at Nazareth.

18. Say a Hail Mary in honour of St. Gabriel, who brought it to earth.

19. Practise some little mortification at meals.

20. Before going to sleep, place yourself with the Infant Jesus in Mary's arms.

21. Say seven Glorias with extended arms, in honour of her Seven Dolours.

22. Make a spiritual communion in union with her dispositions at the Annunciation.

23. Say a Memorare to obtain Mary's help at the hour of death.

24. Keep silence for a short time, and with Mary ponder on God's words in your heart.

25. Say a Hail Mary before going to bed, to prevent one mortal sin during that night.

26. Visit her altar or image in atonement for the desecration of her sanctuaries in England.

27. Say nine Hail Marys in union with the nine choirs of angels who are ever praising her.

28. Say a Salve for the spread of devotion to her.

29. Say fifteen Glorias, in honour of the last fifteen years of Mary's life, for the grace of perseverance.

30. Kiss the ground, and say three Hail Marys for the virtue of holy purity.

31. Say a Hail Mary in reparation for your neglect of Mary's service during this month.

LIFE OF MARY.

1. Predestination. Reverence for God's Mother.
2. Immaculate Conception. Inward Holiness.
3. Nativity. Cheerfulness of Heart.
4. Presentation. Self-sacrifice.
5. Espousals. Sanctification of Daily Duties.
6. Annunciation. Correspondence to Grace.
7. Visitation. Visiting the Sick.
8. Doubt of S. Joseph. Patience under reproach.
9. Expectation. Holy Desires.
10. Journey to Bethlehem. Love of Humiliation.
11. The Midnight Cave. Holy Poverty.
12. Purification. The Light of a Good Life.
13. Simeon's Prophecy. Remembrance of the Passion.
14. Flight into Egypt. Avoiding Occasions of Sin.
15. Three Days' Loss. Perseverance under Trials.
16. Finding in the Temple. Visiting B. Sacrament.
17. The Holy Family. Love of Obscurity.
18. Jesus at Nazareth. Holy Obedience.
19. The Marriage at Cana. Confidence in Prayer.
20. Public Life. Hearing Sermons.
21. Jesus with the Cross. Hatred of Sin.
22. Crucifixion. Daily Mass.
23. Descent from the Cross. Devotion S. Heart.
24. Entombment. Dread of losing Jesus.
25. Mary with the Apostles. Heavenly Wisdom.
26. Resurrection. Joy in Christ's Service.
27. Ascension. Unselfish Aims.
28. Pentecost. Devotion to the Holy Ghost.
29. Death. Conformity to God's Will.
30. Assumption. Frequent Thought of Heaven.
31. Coronation. Love of the Church.

First Day.
Predestination.

It pleased God, in Himself all-sufficient and supremely happy, to decree the creation of men and angels, who should be endowed with their several perfections of nature and grace, and share with Him the joys of heaven. And though, in the order of nature, angels, being pure spirits, rank next to Him, yet in the order of grace He so loved man that, in completing the circle of predestination, He ordained the union of man with God in the person of His only-begotten Son. And to effect this miracle of His love, He willed not to fashion for Himself a body as He did for Adam, but to be conceived and born of a human Mother. Mary therefore was chosen by the Father from all eternity to coöperate with the Holy Ghost in the conception, birth, and training of Jesus, God and man, and to share His work on earth. And as Jesus, the Word made flesh, was to sit at His Father's right hand, so Mary, the Mother of the Word, was predestined to a degree of glory above that of angels and saints, and surpassed only by the glory of her Son. Again, as Jesus, by right of the hypostatic union, was necessarily all-holy, so Mary, by reason of her divine maternity, was rightly endowed with the choicest gifts of nature and grace; and her mighty soul, according to the divine decrees, was to advance from grace to grace till she should be fitted to ascend her mediatorial throne.—*Mater Creatoris, ora pro nobis.*

Reverence for God's Mother.

God has exalted Mary above all creatures, so in your heart and soul she must reign supreme after Him. Consider what is wanting in your reverence or love.

'The Mother of God is the ladder of heaven. God came down to earth by this ladder, that men might by Mary climb up to Him in heaven.'— *S. Fulgentius.*

Fr. Heath, the Franciscan martyr, when a Protestant student at Cambridge, went up to London to be reconciled to the Church. He searched, however, in vain for a priest; for the Catholics to whom he applied turned him away as a spy. In despair, he bethought him of Mary's prayers, and, kneeling down in the street, he, for the first time, invoked her aid. As he prayed, Mr. Jernyngham, one of those who had just repelled him, came up, accosted him kindly, and took him to a priest, by whom he was received into the Church. Ever after, Fr. Heath trusted wholly to Mary's prayers. Our Lady bestowed on him numberless graces. Among the rest, she so moved his father's heart that, at the age of eighty, the feeble old man crossed to Douay, abjured his heresy at his son's feet, and became a lay-brother in the Franciscan Order.

'I was set up from eternity, and of old before the earth was made.'—Prov. viii. 23.

Second Day.
Immaculate Conception.

THE gracious design of God was marred by the sin of man, yet the very terms of the curse declared that a Redeemer should come ; and that as by woman sin had triumphed, so by woman sin should be destroyed. Four thousand years passed, and every human child entered life an enemy of God and a slave of Satan. At length came the hour of the promise. The King of Heaven was to descend on earth, and the first and fullest recipient of His royal bounty was to be the Mother He chose. Being destined, not only to the highest holiness, but, as His Mother, to have God within her in a manner shared by none, she was redeemed, not only more fully than others, but in a higher way. She, and she alone, of Adam's children was exempt from Adam's curse. In the first instant of its creation, her soul, preserved from original sin, was adorned with supernatural justice, the plenitude of sanctifying grace, and a most ample dower of virtues. At once purified and perfected, with the full use of reason, Mary turned to God, and adored Him as her Creator with heart, mind, and will. Never did she lie under the curse of sin ; 'her foundations were on the holy mountains.' She, 'the only perfect one,' began where others end, whether in knowledge or love ; and the first note of her lifelong *Magnificat* was sung when she was conceived immaculate.—*Sancta Virgo virginum, ora pro nobis.*

Inward Holiness.

Learn from Mary Immaculate the holiness which God requires in those whom He chooses as His own. Pray Him to cleanse you more and more from the least stain of sin, and add your own endeavour.

'Simple and chaste should be those eyes which are accustomed to behold the Body of Christ.'— *Imitation.*

The purity of B. John Berchmans' soul beamed so brightly from his face, that persons passing him in the streets would stop to ask his prayers. As a child he had vowed to live a virgin for Mary's sake, and thenceforth he kept his senses sealed to things of earth. During his three years in Rome he never raised his eyes to witness any spectacle, save that of Corpus Christi. He never passed our Lady's statue without saluting it, nor left a church without visiting her altar. Every meal before tasting food, and at night before composing himself to sleep, he said a Hail Mary in honour of the Immaculate Conception; and to this practice he ascribed his exemption from all temptations of the flesh. He invented a Rosary in honour of that mystery, and made a vow, signed with his blood, ever to defend its truth. At the age of twenty-two he was already ripe for heaven, and went to his reward.

'All the glory of the King's daughter is within.' —Ps. xliv. 14.

Third Day.
Nativity.

JOACHIM and Anne, the parents of Mary, came from an illustrious line of chosen servants of God. They were saints themselves; and in their old age, as a special answer to prayer, Mary was born. All creatures claimed a share in the joy of that hour. The angels rejoiced in the birth of one more God-like than Lucifer, who was to crush the rebel chief and reign over them in his stead. Men rejoiced, for the flesh of Mary, of like substance with their own, was to become the flesh of Jesus, in whom they were to be born anew to the life of grace, and be once more heirs of heaven. The earth, with all upon it, had been placed under Adam's dominion, to use, not for himself, but for God; and after his sin creatures ministered no more to their Maker's glory, but to the passions of fallen man. Under this servitude they groaned and travailed, till, by the advent of Mary Immaculate, they were restored to their original purpose before God. All things were renewed and made glad — the manifold life and beauty of hill, plain, and forest. But whatever in nature was stately and fair—the cedar of Lebanon and the cypress on Sion, the rose of Saron and the lily of the field—feebly typified the perfection of the sinless infant, the second world which God had created for His own dwelling-place. The reign of darkness was ended, for the morning-star had risen which preceded the 'Sun of Justice' and announced the eternal day.— *Stella matutina, ora pro nobis.*

Cheerfulness of Heart.

God alone is the source of true joy. Learn to despise the world's deceitful joys, and to refresh your soul by the contemplation of Mary, God's perfect work.

'Thy nativity, O Mary, has announced joy to the whole world.'—*Roman Breviary*.

S. Bernardine of Siena, when preaching to his townsmen on September 8th, the feast of Mary's Nativity, told them that on that day he had been born, had entered the Order of S. Francis, made his solemn profession, sung his first Mass, preached his first sermon, and that for the love and grace of Mary he hoped to die thereon. Our Lady had, by a miracle, cured a complaint of his throat, which prevented his preaching; and the saint ever after used his voice to declare the glory of Mary and of her Divine Son. During his ministry he succeeded in establishing some three hundred houses of the strict observance, which he dedicated to S. Maria di Gesù, to record his trust in these holy names. Under the heaviest trials he was never sad, but won men's hearts by his bright and joyous spirit. This grace he attributed, with every other blessing of his life, to his constant meditation on Mary's seven earthly joys, and to the Rosary he recited in their honour.

'And my spirit hath rejoiced in God my Saviour.'—Luke i. 47.

Fourth Day.
Presentation.

'HEARKEN, daughter, and see, and incline thine ear, and forget thy people and thy father's house.' So spoke David; and Mary, his true daughter, was the first who fully heard and obeyed. She was but three years old when God called her to leave her home. She loved her parents tenderly, and was the joy of their old age; nevertheless at once she set forth. Joachim and Anne accompanied her, and their sorrow made her sacrifice all the more generous. Alone Mary mounted the Temple steps, knelt before Zachary the priest, and, first of her sex, consecrated by vow her virginity to God. Then she passed into the inner court, apart from men's sight. In her cloistered life she strove to be in night-watching foremost, in learning most skilled, in singing psalms most exact, in submission most humble. All her words were full of grace, yet she spoke little with her companions. With the angels who ministered to her she held constant converse. The Holy Spirit taught her the secrets of the Divine Word, and she acquired that habit of pondering thereon which the Gospel twice records. In the precincts of the sanctuary Mary grew and matured in holiness, like a flower of the forest, unseen. Day and night, in work or prayer, she renewed her vow, and gave herself more perfectly to God. Even in sleep her heart watched, listening for the voice of her Beloved, whom she had chosen as her portion for ever.—*Rosa mystica, ora pro nobis.*

Self-Sacrifice.

Consider at what an early age and how completely Mary dedicated herself to God; and think with shame on your own tardy and imperfect conversion.

'Give your soul to God a thousand times a day.'
—*S. Francis of Sales.*

When S. Catherine of Siena was but five years old, she showed her devotion to our Lady by often mounting the stairs on her knees, and saying a Hail Mary on each step. At six years of age a glorious vision of Jesus Christ enraptured her soul, and from that hour she accounted the pleasures of earth as dirt and dung in comparison to the love of her sweet Lord. She now longed to consecrate her virginity to Him; and, remembering that Mary was the first to do so, she asked her what way she might best take for His greater glory and her own soul's health. And our Lady, through whom the longing was first planted in her heart, answered her request by quickening the desire, and instructing her how to carry it out. In a secret part of the house Catherine then knelt down, and pledged her faith and promise to Jesus and Mary, and vowed by His help to keep herself a true and undefiled virgin to Him alone.

'Mary hath chosen the best part, which shall not be taken from her.'—Luke x. 42.

Fifth Day.
Espousals.

WHEN our Blessed Lady had spent eleven years in the Temple, she reached the age at which Jewish maidens were given in marriage. It was God's will, in order to conceal the mystery of the Incarnation, that Mary also should be espoused. Joachim and Anne were dead, and upon the priests fell the duty of choosing a husband. They selected Joseph the son of Jacob, a carpenter of Nazareth, who was known in his daily life as 'a just man' and virtuous. He was of the same tribe and family as Mary, and was therefore of the royal house of David. Like Mary, he had vowed to live a virgin, and was thus fitted to be her earthly guardian, and to shield her good name. Mary, by divine inspiration, accepted Joseph as her husband, and went home with him. In their house at Nazareth Joseph treated her with the utmost reverence, and her life was as hidden as in the Temple. She never went abroad without need, but pursued in secret her prayer and ardent sighing for Christ. She was endowed with more than angelic knowledge, and enriched beyond all creatures with the highest privileges of grace; nevertheless to Joseph, as her husband and head, Mary showed most ready and loving submission. The one 'valiant woman,' she knit and span for herself and the household, and ministered personally to all. She neglected nothing, forgot nothing, and discharged to the moment every duty, though in heart remaining present with God.—*Vas honorabile, ora pro nobis.*

Sanctification of Daily Duties.

Strive like Mary to fulfil faithfully, and for God, the ordinary duties of your state, even those which may be repugnant to you.

'For with God nothing, however trifling, done for God's sake, will go unrewarded.'—*Imitation.*

S. Edmund had been trained by his mother in a tender devotion to our Blessed Lady. When twelve years old, being sent to study at Oxford, he found himself exposed to new and grave temptations. He saw but one mode of escape: entering the church of our Lady, and kneeling before her image, he placed one ring on its finger and another on his own, and thus took Mary for his bride. Of a gentle and retiring nature, he was promoted against his will to the see of Canterbury, where, in the simple discharge of his duty, he endured slander, persecution, and exile; but he was faithful till death. Love of Mary was the secret of his strength. He fasted on her feasts, visited her altar every night, wore a hair-shirt in her honour every Wednesday, had her image before him as he studied, and when he lay down to rest wrote the name of Mary on his forehead and heart. Her image smiled on him as he died, and the ring of his espousals was found on his finger in death.

'He hath done all things well.'—Mark vii. 37.

Sixth Day.
Annunciation.

IN the silence of midnight the Archangel Gabriel was sent from heaven to the lowly room at Nazareth, where Mary was praying. He saluted her as full of grace, and bade her fear not, for she should conceive and bring forth a Son, and call His name Jesus. On her reply hung the world's salvation. The glorious seraph knelt before the earthly maiden, and God awaited her consent. But Mary said, 'How shall this be done, because I know not man?' The angel answered, 'The Holy Ghost shall come upon thee, and the power of the Most High shall overshadow thee; therefore also the Holy, to be born of thee, shall be called Son of God.' Then Mary, certain of remaining a virgin, although a mother, accepted the message of grace. 'Behold the handmaid of the Lord,' she said; 'be it done to me according to thy word.' *And the Word was made flesh.*

For, as God's command created heaven and earth; as the priest's word changes bread into the Body of Christ; so, by Mary's fiat, the Holy Spirit was brought down from the bosom of the Father to the centre of her immaculate heart. In that moment He espoused her, and of her most pure blood a living body was formed, which the Eternal Word in the same instant assumed. Thus in the fulness of time God sent His Son, made of a woman. The Virgin had conceived; Mary was the Mother of God.—*Mater divinæ gratiæ, ora pro nobis.*

Correspondence to Grace.

Readily respond to any call of grace, however high. Faithful correspondence produces God in you, and fortifies you to carry out whatever He calls you to do.

———

'The life of the just man is not the work of man, but of God, or rather of God and man: of God by the operation of grace, of man by the coöperation of obedience.'—*S. Augustine.*

———

S. Ignatius arose one night from his bed of sickness, and, flinging himself on his knees before an image of our Lady, offered himself at once and for ever to Jesus, through her hands. As he did so the house was violently shaken, showing thereby God's acceptance of the sacrifice and the corresponding rage of hell. A vision of Mary and the Infant Jesus perfected his conversion and purified his heart for ever. On his recovery, he set out for Monserrat. There, on the vigil of the Annunciation, at the altar of Mary, Ignatius hung up his sword and dagger, and, clad as a poor pilgrim, watched and prayed till break of day. Then he received Holy Communion, and, staff in hand, bareheaded, with his wounded foot still bandaged, he went forth in the strength of Jesus to found the Society which bears that sacred name.

———

'Speak, Lord, for Thy servant heareth.'—1 Kings iii. 9.

Seventh Day.
Visitation.

IN becoming the Mother of Jesus, Mary was called to abandon her loved seclusion, and to labour for the salvation of men. A few days, therefore, after S. Gabriel's message, she rose with haste to leave Nazareth, and visit her cousin Elizabeth, then six months with child. The journey was a long one of about a hundred miles over the mountains of Judea; but it was the first mission of the Word Incarnate on earth, and Mary's charity levelled the high hills and smoothed the rough ways. She arrived at the house of Zachary, and with all humility was the first to salute her cousin. A fount of sanctifying grace streamed forth with her words, and, penetrating to the soul of the unborn infant, cleansed it from original sin, and told that Christ had come. Then, as he awoke to reason and became conscious of the presence of Jesus, his whole frame thrilled with joy, and he leapt in his mother's womb. Thus S. John became the herald of his Lord, and Elizabeth his mother was filled with the Holy Ghost. With a loud voice she proclaimed Mary blessed among women and blessed the fruit of her womb,—blessed in believing what the angel had told her, most blessed as the Mother of God. And amidst these, the highest and truest praises ever bestowed on a creature, Mary divested herself of all honour and ascribed all to God, saying, ' My soul doth magnify the Lord.'—*Salus infirmorum, ora pro nobis.*

Visiting the Sick.

Break off prayer or any occupation for your suffering neighbour's sake; but, like Mary, have Christ with you whithersoever you go.

'Be assured that nothing brings so much consolation and sweetness to souls that love God as leaving Christ for Christ.'—*S. Philip Neri.*

S. Philip Neri took a most tender care of his penitents, and when they were sick he visited them day and night. He used to teach them short ejaculations to Mary for their comfort and strength, and his visits and prayers brought such peace to the sufferers, that one of his own sons said he had never known what Philip's power was till he came to die. In 1594, Philip, then in his seventy-ninth year, lay, as it seemed, at the very point of death. Suddenly his body was raised up in the air, and he began to exclaim, weeping most tenderly, 'O my most holy Madonna, my beautiful Madonna, I am not worthy; for who am I that you should come to see me and take away my pain? and what shall I do if I get well—I, who have never yet done any good?' Then when he came to himself, and saw that others were present, he covered his face with the sheet and burst into tears. Our Lady's visit had restored him to perfect health.

'The charity of Christ presseth us.'—2 Cor. v. 14.

Eighth Day.
Doubt of S. Joseph.

MARY remained with her cousin about three months. On her return home a heavy trial awaited her. She had been openly greeted by S. Elizabeth as the Mother of the Lord, yet God so willed that he who was nearest to her of all creatures, S. Joseph, her spouse and the chosen guardian of her virginity, should remain ignorant of the miracle which had taken place. When, therefore, he saw that she was about to become a mother, his soul was wrung with doubt and grief. He could not suspect her purity, for each day revealed some fresh example of holiness; yet neither could he doubt the fact which was before his eyes. He felt there was a mystery known to her, but hidden from him; and, as he was both most gentle and most just, he thought to leave her secretly and retire to some distant land. Our Lady saw the daily anguish of his suspense, and felt his sufferings as her own. Yet she spoke not. The miracle wrought within her was the work of God alone. The secret was His, not hers; to Him she left the hour of its revelation, and with it the care of her honour and the consolation of her spouse. Silently, humbly, and steadfastly she persevered in prayer, till God sent an angel to Joseph, and bade him 'Fear not to take unto him Mary his wife, for that of the Holy Ghost she had conceived; and her Son was to be called Jesus, for He should save His people from their sins.'—*Mater purissima, ora pro nobis.*

Patience under Reproach.

When justice is not done to you, suffer and be silent. Lay your case in secret before God, and He will turn all things to your good.

'What folly is this, O my God? Why are we so concerned at being falsely accused by all men, if we are innocent before Thee?'—*S. Teresa.*

S. Isidore, the ploughman, and his pious wife, Mary Toribia, agreed, after the death of their first child, to live together in holy chastity. They were both most devout to our Lady, and Mary undertook charge of the lamp at her shrine near their cottage, on the other side of the river Xarama. A wicked neighbour suggested to Isidore that his wife's frequent visits to the shrine were but an excuse to enable her to meet secretly a herdsman of those parts. Isidore concealed himself to watch her movements. He saw her come down to the river, which proved too swollen for her to ford. Unconscious of his presence, Mary made the sign of the Cross on the torrent; then spreading her cloak upon the waters, she stepped upon it, and was carried dry-shod to the other bank, with the burning lamp in her hand. Isidore had seen enough: he went home, thanking God and our Lady for having given him a saint for his wife.

'Casting all your care upon Him, for He hath care of you.'—1 Peter v. 7.

Ninth Day.
Expectation.

AGE after age the figure of the Messias had been more fully portrayed, and at each step in revelation the men whom God loved most were known as 'men of desires.' In Mary, supreme wisdom and love kindled the desire of the Messias to an absorbing intensity. She knew better than psalmist or prophet that He was to be beautiful beyond the sons of men, and that grace was poured forth on those lips which she was soon to press to her own. She longed to call Him by the name 'above every other name,' which was to blot out the stain of sin, open the gates of Limbus, and bind the powers of hell. As prophet after prophet had long watched for the glimmer of the dawn, now Mary counted the days and hours till the Sun of Justice should arise. Already she had known the Baptist leap with joy at His approach. Daily she was being sanctified by each throb of His Sacred Heart. No more by faith alone, but by sense and touch her heart and her flesh rejoiced in the living God. One thing only was wanting—to behold as a mother and to worship as a creature the face of her Christ. With loving care she made ready for His coming; she prepared the linen bands which were to bind the Eternal; and each day her desire grew more ardent, as she awaited the moment, hastened by her sighs, when the mystery of ages should be accomplished, and the Expected of nations should be given to men.
—*Regina Prophetarum, ora pro nobis.*

Holy Desires.

Be not content with now and then wishing to be holy, but kindle and renew your desires each day. You will thus not only intend, but do.

'The whole life of a Christian is one continued desire.'—*S. Augustine.*

B. John Leonardi, from his earliest childhood, longed to be a priest, but his poverty and ignorance seemed hopeless obstacles. Yet he never despaired. He confided his wish to our Lady, and did what he could to grow in sanctity. While he was assistant to a chemist at Lucca, his fervour was such that he was allowed to communicate daily. After the shop was closed he would go twice or thrice a week to Pisa, ten miles distant, to assist at the exercises of the Brotherhood to which he belonged. At the age of twenty-six, Leonardi was at last enabled to begin his studies, and, after many trials, was finally ordained priest in 1572. His piety drew round him other young men, with whom he founded the Congregation of the Mother of God. To our Lady's prayers he attributed the blessed fulfilment of his hopes; and forty years' incessant persecution and suffering only deepened his trust in Mary, and kindled the desire to behold her face to face.

'He hath filled the hungry with good things.'
—Luke i. 53.

Tenth Day.
Journey to Bethlehem.

IN the bitter cold of December, Mary and Joseph set out from Nazareth for Bethlehem, to be enrolled in the census which the Roman Emperor had ordered. The village was eighty miles distant, but it was the home of David their ancestor, and there alone must their names be inscribed. Each step of the road recalled memories of the past: the mountain pass, where Judith showed herself 'the glory of Israel and the joy of her people;'—the vale of Sichem, where Abraham raised his first altar in the land promised to his seed, and where still is the well of Jacob;—Bethel, now truly a sanctuary by the presence of Mary, herself the house of God and the gate of heaven. It was the fourth or fifth day before the pilgrims ascended, by the fields where Ruth had gleaned and David kept his flocks, to the hill village of Bethlehem. The place was full of strangers, and rang with the sounds of mirth and feasting. Mary and Joseph were wayworn and faint, and her state as a mother alone merited pity; but they were poor and unknown; and scornful refusal was the only welcome for the Son of David and His royal parents, as they wandered from house to house for shelter this keen winter's night. They toiled on to a lowly stable on the hill-side, and there, with the ox and the ass for companions, the Mother of the Messias awaited the birth of her God.—*Turris Davidica, ora pro nobis.*

Love of Humiliation.

All Christians profess humility, but few bear humiliations. Learn to value each one as a preparation for some great grace. It was after bearing insult and hardship that Mary brought forth her Son.

———

'Strive to become little with the Little One, that you may increase in stature with Him.'— *S. Bonaventure.*

———

B. Benedict Joseph Labre left home and parents to live as a poor beggar near the sanctuaries of Jesus and Mary. His ragged and miserable state procured for him insults and blows; and he was turned out of the church itself as a hypocrite and vagabond. But the presence of Jesus in the tabernacle warmed his heart, and the thought of Mary turned his sorrows to joy. He wore her rosary round his neck. Her shrine at Loreto was his favourite pilgrimage, her picture at Santa Maria dei Monti his chosen spot for prayer. There he would spend hours rapt in devotion, unconsciously edifying all around him; while the words, 'O Mary, O my Mother!' would burst from his lips. There he knelt for the last time in prayer, and thence his soul made its last pilgrimage to Mary and to God.

———

'He hath put down the mighty from their seat; He hath exalted the humble.'—Luke i. 52.

Eleventh Day.
The midnight Cave.

NINE months had gone by since the surpassing merits of Mary had drawn Jesus from the bosom of His Father to make her heart His home; and now again, in the silence of midnight, her soul was filled with peace unutterable, when, in answer to her heart's desire, He issued forth from her bosom, and lay before her on the ground. First of all creatures Mary looked upon the face of the Incarnate Word, and adored the Babe, helpless and mute, as her Creator and God. Then, as He shivered and wept with the cold, she pressed Him to her bosom, wrapped His trembling limbs in swaddling clothes, and laid Him in a manger. By that sign angels taught the shepherds to know and adore Him. Thither three Wise Men from the East came, despising the court of Herod, to bring the royal gifts of gold, frankincense, and myrrh. These were His by right. He was truly King of of kings as well as Saviour. Nevertheless, He lacked the bare necessaries of life. Mary knew that this want and poverty were His own free choice, and that 'He had robbed Himself of His glory for our sake, that through His poverty we might be rich.' She gave therefore to the poor the costly offerings, and kept for her Child and herself the straw, the manger, and the rough cave; preferring to live on what friends might give in alms, and the chance toil of S. Joseph might procure.—*Mater inviolata, ora pro nobis.*

Holy Poverty.

For the love of Christ's poor, deprive yourself of some comfort, and thereby lay up treasure in heaven.

'Poverty is the way of salvation, the nurse of humility, and the root of perfection. Its fruits are hidden, but they are multiplied in endless ways.'—*S. Francis.*

S. Francis had already given up home and riches for Christ. He was one day in the church of S. Mary of the Angels, which he had repaired with his own hands, and heard the Gospel, 'Possess neither scrip for your journey, nor two coats, nor shoes, nor staff.' He rejoiced to find that he could yet strip himself of something for the love of Christ. He gave away his shoes, his staff, and pilgrim's garb, and clad himself in one worn-out tunic girt with a cord. Then he began to preach; disciples flocked to him, and S. Mary of the Angels became the cradle and sanctuary of the great Franciscan Order. The church was of the poorest kind, but it had treasures of its own. For there, in answer to the prayers of Mary, Jesus in person granted to S. Francis the celebrated indulgence of the Portiuncula, which enriches the faithful in every age.

'Blessed are ye poor, for yours is the kingdom of God.'—Luke vi. 20.

Twelfth Day.
Purification.

ON the fortieth day after the Nativity, Mary went up to the Temple to present her Child according to the law. At the same time she humbled herself before men, by submitting to the rite of purification, which was appointed for the mothers of a fallen race. In that Temple she had spent twelve years of her spotless life. There, too, she had publicly accomplished the vow, which she had made in the moment of her conception, and dedicated her virginity to God. Now she is returning to it a virgin still, but, by a miracle of grace, a mother bearing a child. There was nothing singular in the outward semblance of Mary and Jesus as they entered the sacred court. Yet when Simeon gazed on the Child, whom Mary laid in his arms, he saw before him the one object of his prayer, his hopes, and his life, the Lord's Christ. The sight was heaven to him, and in this foretaste of its joy he lifted his voice in praise, and declared he would die in peace, for 'his eyes had seen the salvation of God—a light to the revelation of the Gentiles, and the glory of His people Israel.' Thus did the Lord, so long sought for, come to His Temple; and Mary wondered at the words, sublime and deep, by which God made known the glory of her Child, and caused her own light to break forth in the hour when it seemed most hidden.—*Speculum justitiæ, ora pro nobis.*

The Light of a Good Life.

You are bound as a Christian, besides saving your own soul, to edify your neighbour. Scrupulously fulfil the least precept of Holy Church, and you will satisfy this twofold duty.

'Let us follow Christ, the true Light, and walk no more in darkness. But the darkness to be dreaded is of life, not of sight.'—*S. Augustine.*

Blessed Henry Suso used to prepare a triple taper for three days before Candlemas; the first taper was in token of Mary's purity, the second of her humility, the third of her divine maternity. And he prepared this spiritual candle daily with three *Magnificats*. On the morning of the feast he went early to the church, and waited her coming in contemplation before the high altar. In spirit he met her at the outer gate, with countless loving souls, and sang with voiceless melody the prose *Inviolata*, 'O spotless one.' Then he followed with his spiritual candle, praying that she would never permit the divine light to be extinguished within him. After this, by Mary's leave, he most tenderly caressed and worshipped the Divine Child; and, going with her to the Temple, purified his soul from every earthly desire by the love of Jesus Christ.

'You were once darkness, but now light in the Lord. Walk as children of the light.'—Ephes. v. 8.

Thirteenth Day.
Prophecy of Simeon.

A HOLY joy filled the soul of Mary when Simeon broke forth into his canticle of praise at the sight of the Infant Jesus, and in God's Temple and before the crowd of faithful worshippers declared that the Messias had come. Yet in a moment other words were uttered in Mary's ear which changed her joy to sorrow. This same Child, the glory of Israel and the light of the world, would, in His contradictions, sufferings, and death, be a sword piercing her heart. She had known from her study of the Holy Scriptures that, as the Mother of the Saviour, she must suffer herself for men; but she had now a vision clear and detailed of what those sufferings should be. Jesus was to be a butt for the malice of all that was evil on earth and in hell. He was to be called a fool, a glutton, a heretic, a blasphemer, a devil, and mad, and His own people would seek His life. At last He would be mocked, scourged, and spat upon; then set up on Calvary to suffer and die. Then, and for ever after, this vision was before Mary's soul, imprinting its features on Jesus and embittering her love. The swathing bands seemed now the cords of Gethsemani, the milk from her breast a foretaste of the vinegar and gall, each cry of His infancy an echo of the last loud cry when He should give up the ghost. Thus did the sword enter Mary's heart and the sorrow of her life begin.—*Mater Salvatoris, ora pro nobis.*

Constant Thought of the Passion.

Ask Mary that you may keep the Passion ever present in your heart, as it was in hers, by day and night. If you forget it for a moment you may be lost.

───

'Rest in the Passion of Christ, and love to dwell within His sacred wounds.'—*Imitation*.

───

S. Veronica Giuliani, as a child of three years, climbed up to an image of Mary to take Jesus from her arms. Our Lady promised He should be her spouse, and Veronica became a Capuchin nun. Beholding in a vision Christ wounded and bleeding, she offered herself to suffer with Him. A ring of betrothal marked the acceptance of her oblation. At first she drew back in horror from the chalice of the Passion which was presented to her. But love prevailed, and for her remaining thirty-five years she was a living image of Jesus crucified. In body as well as soul she trod every step of the Passion. She was bound, scourged, and crucified, insulted by creatures, and apparently abandoned by God. She was pierced with the five wounds and the crown of thorns. This share in the pains of Jesus taught her such horror of sin, that, although innocent as an angel, she said she should go to hell unless she changed her life.

───

'I judged myself to know nothing but Jesus Christ, and Him crucified.'—1 Cor. ii. 2.

Fourteenth Day.
Flight into Egypt.

AFTER her Purification, our Blessed Lady returned to Nazareth, hoping there, in spite of Simeon's prophecy, to find rest for a while; yet even her obscure home offered no safety. An angel appeared to Joseph in sleep, and bade him fly with Mary and Jesus to Egypt, as Herod was seeking the Child's life. Nothing was told them as to their security on the journey, or means of subsistence and length of stay in the heathen land. Mary thought only of God's will, announced to her through S. Joseph. At his first word, without a murmur or question, she arose, and, taking Jesus in her arms, set forth. A wild road of two hundred miles and the desert lay before her. She was young and delicate, and needed food, shelter, and repose; but the life of Jesus was in danger, and she dared not turn or rest. Ages since, across these same sands, the camp of Israel had marched with the ark of God in their midst, on their way to the land of promise; now the Creator Himself was being borne in the arms of Mary, the living ark, a fugitive from Canaan, to make Egypt His home. And the pagan land paid homage to the true God. Idols broke of themselves as the Eternal Truth passed by, and the palm-trees bent their branches to feed Him with their fruit. At length, at Heliopolis, the Holy Family found shelter, and were able to dwell in safety till the angel announced that Herod was dead.—*Fœderis arca, ora pro nobis.*

Avoiding Occasions of Sin.

Learn from Mary's example not to expect God to work a miracle to save you, but, when warned of danger, save yourself by speedy flight.

'Fly at once, fly far, fly always. Do this, and thou shalt live.'—*S. Philip Neri.*

A young Egyptian woman, known for her beauty and scandalous life, was about to enter a church at Jerusalem, along with other pilgrims. To her horror she found herself held back, while the others passed in. The sense of her shame now burst upon her. Looking up, she saw above the door the picture of the Mother of God. With many tears she begged Mary to have pity on her, and received the answer, 'Pass beyond the Jordan, and there find rest.' She did as she was told. She fled into the depth of the desert, and for forty-seven years saw no human creature nor aught that could remind her of her sins. There the Abbot Zosimus found her, purified and ready for death. She said that to the Mother of God she owed her conversion, flight, and perseverance, and begged that the name of Mary, her protectress, might be written on her grave. This was done, and the holy penitent is honoured in the Church as S. Mary of Egypt.

'Depart from the unjust, and evils shall depart from thee.'—Ecclus. vii. 2.

Fifteenth Day.
Three Days' Loss.

FIVE years had passed since the Holy Family had returned from Egypt to Nazareth, when they went up to Jerusalem, as was their custom, for the Pasch. Jesus from a child had become a boy. He could speak and act for Himself, and the change had made Him dearer than ever to His Mother's heart. The feast lasted a week; and on the eve of the seventh day Mary and Joseph left the Temple by different routes, to meet again, as was usual, at the halting-place on their homeward journey. Each thought that Jesus was with the other; it was only when they met at night that they found He was gone. Neither could explain His absence. He was of all sons the most obedient: now He had left them without a word, though He knew that His loss must wound them to the heart. They could only turn back and search for Him among their friends; and three nights and days Mary wandered through the streets of Jerusalem asking for her Child. But all was in vain; with each fruitless question her fears increased. Had He already begun to teach, and left His home for ever, or was He seized by Archelaus and now hanging on the Cross? Mary could not tell. She was left desolate in utter darkness—a mother deserted by her child, and that child her God. No heavenly guide appeared to direct her steps; yet she never complained, but continued to search and pray till God might send her help.—*Turris eburnea, ora pro nobis.*

Perseverance under Trials.

God hides Himself to make us humble, and to teach us our own misery, that we may learn to lean upon Him even when He seems most hidden.

'When consolation shall be taken away from thee, do not presently despair; but with humility and patience await the heavenly visitation.'—*Imitation.*

When S. Francis of Sales was leading a most holy life as a young student in Paris, he suddenly lost all sensible fervour, and found himself beset by an overpowering temptation to despair. He had always loved God with his whole heart, and now he felt doomed to hate and curse the same God for all eternity. His friends attributed his sadness to love, and tried in vain to divert him. After a month of utter misery he entered the church where he had vowed his virginity to God, and took up a tablet which hung at our Lady's altar. It contained the *Memorare.* The words gave him new courage; and he begged of Mary the grace to love God at least in this life, if he could not do so in the next; and that even in hell, if such might be his fate, he might not curse, but bless His holy name. And as he prayed to his dearest Lady, the dark temptation melted away, and the light of God's presence returned to fill his soul with peace.

'After darkness I hope for light again.'—Job xvii. 12.

Sixteenth Day.
Finding in the Temple.

IT was on the third day that our Lady and S. Joseph, having in vain searched for Jesus among their kinsfolk and friends, bent their steps to the Temple. There a strange sight met their eyes. Through the open door of the hall set apart for teaching they saw the doctors and masters of the law, the most learned men of Israel, gathered in rapt attention round a Boy of twelve years old. Joy and surprise were written on their countenances, as they sought to fathom the sublime doctrine of this new teacher. Even Mary wondered at the simple majesty of her Son, who seemed to her bereaved heart like one risen from the dead. 'My Son,' she said, in loving complaint, 'why hast Thou done this to us? Behold, Thy father and I have sought Thee sorrowing.' She would hide her glory, and call Joseph His father now. He was father before by choice of God, and again by the sorrows and joys which he had shared with her. But Jesus suffered her not to humble herself before men. 'Did you not know,' He said, 'that I must be about My Father's business?' Thus did He declare in His first recorded words, that the Father of Mary's Child, the Father for whom He had left His Mother's side, was none but the Eternal God. Then at once, in obedience to her wish, He left the astonished doctors, and returned with Mary to Nazareth to be the joy of her life.—*Domus aurea, ora pro nobis.*

Visiting the B. Sacrament.

Jesus is ever to be found in the tabernacle. In trial or sorrow look not to men for comfort, but seek Jesus as your friend, and with Him alone will you find peace.

'What can the world give thee without Jesus? To be without Jesus is a grievous hell; to be with Jesus is a sweet paradise.'—*Imitation.*

For forty years S. Felix of Cantalice went round the shops and taverns of Rome, begging alms for his Convent. In spite of much suffering and insult he was always bright and joyous; his common greeting was 'Deo gratias.' Each day on starting he took the hand of his dearest Mother Mary, warning her that if she let him go but once, he must surely fall; and during his round he told his beads, and called her by many sweet names. But it was at night, when alone before the Blessed Sacrament, that he gave full vent to his love; there he would pray for hours, with his arms extended, singing, 'Domine, Domine,' beside himself with joy. One Christmas night he besought his dear Mother to lay her Child for a moment in his arms. Mary did so; and Felix, pressing Jesus to his bosom, fell into an ecstasy, after which he begged to die, for life had no further charm for him.

'Ye shall seek Me, and ye shall find Me, when ye shall seek Me with all your heart.'—Jer. xxix. 13.

Seventeenth Day.
The Holy Family.

WHEN Jesus first taught in the synagogue at Nazareth, the people marvelled at His wisdom and power; but they would not believe, for they said, 'Is not this the carpenter, the Son of Mary?' They had seen Him from childhood daily in their midst; one with them and of them, a poor son of toil. To their mind, He who was so evidently human could never be divine. This obscurity Joseph and His Mother had shared.

Her life was spent in the round of household duties. She visited her friends when charity required, and went up to the Temple for the great feasts; but no priest or prophetess saluted her as blessed. Before men she seemed but the wife of a poor artisan; yet during these years mighty changes were taking place within her. Each day some new and wonderful truth unfolded itself, bringing grace to her soul, as she watched the movements of Jesus, and kept pondering His words in her heart. His whole life was a mystery. There was power in His actions, in His silence, in His retirement, in His rest. He was the light of the world, but a light now concentrated on Mary's heart. Poor as her cottage might seem, it was the one sanctuary of Jehovah on earth, and shone with a glory brighter than rested on the mercy-seat of old—the beauty of the Eternal Holiness, the manifest presence of the living God.—*Virgo prudentissima, ora pro nobis.*

Love of Obscurity.

If you would learn the secrets of Jesus you must, like Mary, seek to live with Him in secret, and to remain hidden from men.

'The soul then only turns to God when it has turned away from the world.'—*S. Augustine.*

S. Germaine Cousin had a deformed right arm, and her face was disfigured by a scrofulous disease. She was kept quite apart from her brothers and sisters, and when she returned home at night from minding the sheep, her stepmother would drive her to the stable to sleep with the cattle. In this strait the little girl turned to our Blessed Lady, and found a true Mother in her. While Germaine each morning withdrew to hear Mass her flock never strayed, nor did the wolves harass it. The children on the hill-side saw a strange light shining on her face as she taught them to tell their beads. Her stepmother tore open her apron, suspecting her of stealing crusts for the poor, but only a shower of heavenly flowers fell to the ground. This miracle got abroad. The poor despised girl was about to be honoured by men; but her humble obscurity had already fitted her for heaven. Germaine was found dead in her stable at the age of twenty-two, and angels were seen escorting her soul on high.

'You are dead, and your life is hid with Christ in God.'—Col. iii. 3.

Eighteenth Day.
Jesus at Nazareth.

WHILE Mary was being instructed by Jesus in the mysteries of His kingdom, He, the All-wise, was showing by daily example how perfect a thing it is to obey. 'He was subject to them.' Such is the sole account the Gospels give of the hidden life at Nazareth. God, before whom angels tremble, was subject to Mary, and to Joseph also for her sake. 'Which is the more wonderful,' asks S. Bernard, 'the condescension of the Son, or the exaltation of the Mother?' For eighteen years Jesus 'learnt no letters;' but having 'taken the form of a slave,' worked in His foster-father's shop, and by the sweat of His brow and task of servile toil gained His daily bread. Time came when Joseph died the happiest death in the arms of Mary and her Son, and Jesus was left the natural head of His earthly home. He had passed from youth to manhood; He was of an age to be freed from His Mother's rule, to do and to teach; still He chose to obey. He preferred to remain in despised Nazareth under His Mother's roof, that He might do what she bade rather than what He would; and this because He knew that Mary alone would never in the least depart from that divine will which He had come on earth to do. And Mary, ever watchful to the promptings of the Holy Spirit, her Spouse, used her authority in such wise that 'Jesus advanced in wisdom and age, and in favour with God and man.'
—*Mater admirabilis, ora pro nobis.*

Holy Obedience.

Dread nothing so much as following your own lights. It is always safer to consider others your superiors, and to do their will rather than your own.

———

'Son, he who striveth to withdraw himself from obedience withdraweth himself from grace.'
—*Imitation.*

———

S. Joseph of Cupertino, being mistrusted on account of his marvellous raptures, was kept in confinement during the last years of his life. Bitter as was the trial, the Saint showed no sign of discontent. He had been trained by our Lady, in her convent of Grottella, to accept cheerfully every command as God's will. When studying for the priesthood, he could only learn one Gospel, '*Beatus venter.*' Under obedience, he presented himself for examination; this Gospel was given him, and he acquitted himself with credit. The mere sight of Mary's image would throw him into an ecstasy; yet one word from the Father Guardian would bring him to himself. At his command, he would exorcise successfully possessed persons, with whom others had failed, by merely reciting the Litany of our Lady, and telling the devils they might go or stay as they would; it was sufficient for him to obey.

———

'Be ye subject therefore to every human creature, for God's sake.'—1 Pet. ii. 13.

Nineteenth Day.
Cana of Galilee.

'THERE was a marriage,' writes S. John, 'in Cana of Galilee; and the Mother of Jesus was there, and Jesus also was invited.' And He who came to bless both the joys and sorrows of human life came also as He was bid. Our Lady was a relative of the host, or had some authority in the house, and when, as it happened, the wine ran short, she pointed it out to Jesus. She saw that such a want would mar the feast and be a reproach to the giver. She knew also, as none other did, the tenderness and power of Him to whom she spoke. 'Woman,' Jesus replied, 'what is it to Me and to thee? Mine hour is not yet come.' He would call her 'Woman,' not 'Mother,' now. It was a divine work for which she pleaded, an act of that divine will which could not be subject to hers. This Mary knew; but she felt assured that what no tie of flesh or blood could claim her prayer would win, and with unfaltering trust she bade the servants do whatsoever He said. Then at His word they filled the empty jars, and drew thence, not the mere water which had been there, but rich and generous wine, the best of all the feast. Thus His hour struck, at His Mother's bidding, and Jesus first shed His glory forth, not to convince the unbelieving, but to 'make joyful the soul and the heart' of Mary's friends.—*Virgo potens, ora pro nobis.*

Confidence in Prayer.

Never doubt that God is ready to help you; but if you would be heard, you must 'do,' as Mary tells us, 'whatsoever He shall say to you.'

Quod Deus imperio, tu prece Virgo potes,—
  'God can all things by behest;
  Thou by prayer, O Virgin blest!'

After many vain attempts to enlist the sympathies of the Emperor Conrad III. and the German nobles in favour of the Crusades, S. Bernard made his final appeal to them in the cathedral of Spires. As the Saint entered the nave the *Salve Regina* was sung, and when its concluding words, '*Post hoc exilium ostende*,' died away, Bernard, as if in rapture, exclaimed, '*O clemens, O pia, O dulcis Virgo Maria.*' The vast congregation was moved by this outburst of devotion. Two days afterwards the Saint preached before the Emperor. Putting his trust in Mary, he boldly upbraided Conrad for his lukewarmness in Christ's cause. His words struck home, and the Emperor and his knights demanded the Cross on the spot. Bernard had healed the sick and raised the dead, but this sudden change of heart was called '*miraculum miraculorum*,' and his inspired words have been added by the Church to the Antiphon of our Lady.

'Open thy mouth wide, and I will fill it.'—Ps. lxxx. 11.

Twentieth Day.
Public Life.

DURING the public life of Jesus, Mary dwelt at Capharnaum, or followed her Son through Galilee and Judea, and ministered to His wants, with other holy women. But her aim was then as ever to keep herself hidden from men. Once only was this humble endeavour defeated, and the whole glory of Jesus was reflected on Mary. In the second year of His ministry a woman in the crowd saw Jesus cure with one word a demoniac, and silence the blasphemous taunts of the Pharisees. Surprised by a scene of such divine power, the woman lifted up her voice, and blessed, with a mother's instinct, not the mighty Teacher Himself, but the Mother who bore Him, and the breasts that gave Him suck. Nor did Jesus reprove her prayer, but He showed that there was a higher blessing even than the divine maternity, which was Mary's as well. 'Yea, rather,' He replied, 'blessed are they who hear the word of God and keep it.' 'She was more blessed,' says S. Augustine, 'in receiving Christ's faith than in conceiving Christ's flesh.' As the Mother of the Word, Mary was exalted above all creatures; but she was dearer to God in keeping the word through perfect obedience, detachment, and virginal purity, than in her relationship to Him. Thus she, whom all generations would bless, was first proclaimed blessed by Him, whose generation was from eternity, the Only-begotten Word.—*Virgo prædicanda, ora pro nobis.*

Hearing Sermons.

Eloquence is useless unless God touches the heart. Say a Hail Mary for the preacher, that the message of God may reach your own and others' hearts.

'He that heareth, if he feareth not, if he is not moved, is not worthy to be healed.'—*S. Augustine.*

S. Alphonso always made his hearers invoke our Lady's aid before he began to preach. At Foggia in 1745 he was extolling the glory of Mary, when an old but miraculous picture of her, which hung in the church, was suddenly lit up, and disclosed full of life and majesty the figure of the Mother of God. At the same moment two brilliant rays from the picture traversed the church, and rested on the head of the Saint, who exclaimed, 'My Queen, would you then give us such joy!' At the end of this mission the entire city was converted, and not one woman of evil life could be found in a population of twenty thousand souls. One only had resisted the Saint's exhortations, and she was suddenly struck dead, without time being given her to repent. The Saint had her body thrown into a public ditch, as a warning to the dull of heart.

'He that hearkeneth to Me shall not be confounded; and they that work by Me shall not sin.'—Ecclus. xxiv. 30.

Twenty-first Day.
Meeting Jesus with the Cross.

WHEN the hour of His sufferings drew near, Jesus went out to Bethany to obtain His Mother's consent to His Passion, and to bid her farewell. Mary knew that His death alone could purchase the salvation of men. She thought not therefore of her own loss, and on her knees before Jesus adored the divine decree. She assisted in spirit at the agony, the trials, and the cruel outrages, but it was on the way to Calvary that she met Him face to face. Only yesterday He had stood before her in the perfect manhood of His three-and-thirty years, with the majesty in form and bearing which had evoked the hosannas and the homage of the whole nation. Today the same multitude cries for His blood. He draws near her, tottering under the weight of the Cross, enfeebled by the scourging, vested in ragged purple, covered with spittle, His head torn with thorns. His Mother's eyes meet His eyes. Dimmed as they are with blood and tears, she may not draw near to wipe them, or to raise Him as He falls. So piteous was the sight that the women standing by beat their breasts and cried aloud; but Mary, though she wept not, saw deeper far. In those hideous wounds and stains she knew the work of sin, the iniquity of evil passions, the malice of men's hearts. In this hour of darkness she united her heart with the Heart of Jesus as a sacrifice for sinners, and followed to suffer with Him.—*Refugium peccatorum, ora pro nobis.*

Increased Hatred of Sin.

Sin to us bears many attractions; yet in truth it is always as Mary saw it, a heartless murderer, crucifying Jesus and slaying our souls. Pray to see it as she did.

'Why add sorrow to the afflicted? More painful to Christ are the wounds of our sins than the wounds of His Body.'—*S. Bernard.*

At the age of eleven S. Aloysius Gonzaga made for himself a belt of sharp spurs, which he wore round his loins till he could obtain a hair-shirt. He restricted his food to the daily allowance of one ounce weight, and he would rise from his father's luxurious table famished and faint with hunger. Under the soft linen of his bed he laid pieces of wood, and on the darkest winter's night he would rise secretly and pray for six long hours, while his limbs stiffened with cold. Then he scourged the shivering flesh till the blood flowed again. To his mother's sorrowful remonstrance he replied, ' Hinder me not from doing thus little for my sins.' A childish theft, one immodest word inadvertently repeated at the age of five years—these were his crimes. But Aloysius was a spouse of Mary, and he saw, as angels see, the least taint of sin.

' I am brought to nothing, and I knew not; I am become as a beast before Thee.'—Ps. lxxii. 22, 23.

Twenty-second Day.
Crucifixion.

It was by Mary's hands that Jesus was first presented in the Temple, and He would have her again with Him on Calvary. He was to die for all men, and to die afresh for every mortal sin. He was to offer Himself in sacrifice for the world, and Mary knew that she, as Mother of the Saviour, was to take part in this oblation. With her whole soul, therefore, she willingly suffered with Jesus laid upon the Cross; she counted each stroke of the hammer, and watched the nails force their way through the Hands and Feet of her Son. She saw the Cross raised, with its living weight, and amid yells and blasphemies driven into its socket with a bound. Earth trembled and the sun was darkened; but under that Cross Mary stood alone, firm and recollected, while the great noonday sacrifice was offered, and her Son hung a willing victim between heaven and earth, till His life-blood ebbed away. Jesus was her very life, her Creator and her Child, the one object of her worship and love; but she would not hold back one drop of His Blood, which was the price of the salvation of men.

'And Jesus saw His Mother, and said, Mother, behold thy Son: and to the disciple, Son, behold thy Mother.' Thus was Mary, not by angel's message, but by the bleeding lips of the Son of God, again proclaimed a mother—mother of all mankind.—*Vas insigne devotionis, ora pro nobis.*

Daily Mass.

Learn from Mary on Calvary so to assist at Holy Mass, that you may die to yourself and live only for God and your neighbour.

'In Mass and Communion I have found, when faint and spent, such courage and strength, that I could give my life for Christ.'—*B. Sebastian Valfré.*

S. Paul of the Cross received from our Lady herself the black habit which his sons were to wear as a badge of the Passion. The outward dress expressed the thought of his heart. If he walked through the fields, the thorns, the nails, the Precious Blood seemed stamped on every blade and leaf. If he saw a chain of pearls worn as an ornament, it told him of the fetters of Christ. The remembrance of Friday was, he said, enough to take life away, and he called his Congregation 'of the Passion,' that its members might have no master but Christ crucified. When he preached, 'A God bound for me, a God scourged for me, a God dying for me,' was his only theme. At Holy Mass his love reached its height. There, in union with Mary, he followed Jesus through each stage of the Passion, and clothed himself anew in the sufferings of Christ, and offered himself for the souls of men.

'Greater charity no man hath than that he lay down his life for his friends.'—John xv. 13.

Twenty-third Day.
Taking down from the Cross.

'CONSUMMATUM est.' Jesus is dead! Yet His lifeless Body is not free from insult. In sheer malice a soldier drives his lance through the Sacred Side. The blow was dealt at Jesus; but Mary's heart was also pierced, and she alone felt the wound. The crowd now disperses, and Calvary is deserted and still. At length Joseph and Nicodemus approach, having obtained leave from Pilate to bury the Body of Jesus. They draw the nails one by one from the Hands and Feet, and the Body, heavy in death, falls forward into their arms. With most tender reverence they lower it to Mary's lap, where it lies helpless and mute as in the first days of infancy. Once more the Mother's care is needed to cleanse the sacred Flesh, and to prepare it for its resting-place. Each member has a special wound, which deepens her sorrow by the tale of suffering it tells. The Eyes which converted Peter, the Hands full of blessings for children, the Breast where John reclined, the Feet the home of the Magdalen — all are torn and defiled by sin. With deepest worship Mary adores every scar and gash as she anoints them with the myrrh and spices which Nicodemus has brought. At length the work is done; and while angels tremble, she binds in swathing bands the Body of her God, and shrouds from an ungrateful world the Face of its Lord Christ.—*Regina martyrum, ora pro nobis.*

Devotion to the Sacred Heart.

Try often to look into the depths of the Sacred Heart, and measure your love of Christ by Christ's love of you.

'The ingratitude of men is more painful to Me than all the sufferings of My Passion.'—*Revelation to B. Margaret Mary.*

When B. Margaret Alacoque learnt in childhood that Jesus is present in the B. Sacrament, she began to spend every leisure moment before the altar; and to pray better, she knelt on her bare knees, gave Mary her heart to keep, and kissed the ground after every Ave she recited. Her first Communion was followed by a sickness of four years, from which she only recovered by promising to consecrate herself to our Lady's service. She entered the Visitation Convent at Paray, and took the name of Mary. Our Lord now told her always to pray and suffer as His Mother did during His Passion. And it was while she was thus praying before the B. Sacrament that He showed her His Sacred Heart, torn and bleeding through the coldness of men. Thus Margaret Mary found herself chosen to be the apostle of the Sacred Heart, and to preach this great work of reparation among men.

'Wheresoever the body shall be, there the eagles will be gathered together.'—Matt. xxiv. 28.

Twenty-fourth Day.
Entombment.

In a garden close by Calvary was a new sepulchre, belonging to Joseph of Arimathea, wherein never man had been laid. To this spot, slowly and in silence, when the shades of evening had set in, the Body of Jesus was borne. Within the hewn rock it was reverently laid, with the instruments of the Passion by its side. Then a great stone was rolled to the opening and the sepulchre was closed. Mary was now without Jesus in the world, a new and most bitter suffering. On Calvary her sorrow had been intense; but her Son, though dying, was still alive, and His voice, when raised in prayer or blessing, had soothed her pain. At the descent from the Cross His dead Body was a companion dearer and more consoling than angels or saints; the mere anointing of His wounds had been a salve of divine healing to her own soul. But now she was alone—alone after thirty-three years of closest union, worship, and love. Jesus had predestined her for Himself. She existed but for Him. Why should she live now that He was dead? For our sakes alone was Mary thus left desolate, that by the throes of her agony she might plead for sinners, and by the cries of her own sharp travail bring us forth again as children of grace. In the hour of temptation, in the presence of sin, 'forget not the groanings of thy Mother.'—*Consolatrix afflictorum, ora pro nobis.*

Dread of losing Jesus.

Fear nothing so much as the loss of Jesus, and remember that the least venial sin or unfaithfulness may end in that loss.

'O Mary, my good Mother, keep me always under thy protection, for if thou leavest me, I shall behave worse than Judas.'—*S. Alphonso Liguori.*

S. Dominic clothed his children in a white habit in honour of Mary's purity, and hung the rosary on their girdle that her name might be ever on their lips. Her image was placed by the crucifix over their beds to guard them as they slept; and the rule prescribed that on first rising they should sing together, before even they were shod, the Office of Mary. In return, our Lady told the Saint that whenever his children together sang the *Salve*, she prostrated herself for them before her Divine Son. One night, in the dormitory of S. Sabina, she appeared in glittering state with S. Catherine and S. Cecilia, and sprinkled with holy water the sleeping friars. From one alone she turned away, and he was left unblest; he was sleeping in an attitude unbecoming a religious man. 'O, what strict discipline,' says the chronicler, 'should we keep, if even unwittingly we may cause our Lady to hide her face!'

'He that contemneth small things shall fall by little and little.'—Ecclus. xix. 1.

Twenty-fifth Day.
Mary with the Apostles.

WHEN Jesus was buried His Mother desired ardently to be left alone in her sorrow, that in secret she might worship His Soul in Limbus and His Body in the grave. But she had been appointed the Mother of men, and the bereaved and doubting Apostles claimed her maternal care. Her first act, therefore, on returning to the upper room, was to bid S. John find S. Peter and bring him to her. No one but Mary could comfort the penitent Apostle; for after Jesus, no one had been so wronged by him. With a wisdom, grace, and tenderness inspired from above, she taught him the love and mercy of Jesus, and showed him how, by the experience of his fall, to grow in mistrust of self, and by reliance upon God to become in very truth 'the rock.' One by one the Apostles gathered to her side, as children round a loving mother, and found in her words divine consolation and strength. She encouraged the desponding Thomas, showed to James and John the nature of that kingdom where they had prayed to reign, and instructed Andrew how to love the Cross. She spoke to all the Apostles, of Jesus, of Bethlehem, and Nazareth, and through renewed faith and love led them to hope and pray for the triumph of Easter morn. Thus was spent the first Christian Saturday, which was henceforth to be venerated as Mary's day; for on it the Apostles were sanctified by Mary's faith, and won to Christ again.— *Sedes sapientiæ, ora pro nobis.*

Heavenly Wisdom.

Learn in doubt and sorrow to seek comfort of Mary. She will obtain for you grace to understand your cross, and so to profit by it.

'Grant me, O Lord, above all things, to relish Thee and to love Thee; and to understand all other things as they are according to the order of Thy wisdom.'—*Imitation.*

In 1280, Blessed Albert the Great, who for forty years had been the light of the schools, was lecturing at Cologne, when he suddenly stopped speaking. After a long pause he thus continued: 'Listen to me, dear sons, and I will tell you something old and new. As a novice I was so dull a scholar, I nearly left my Order in shame. What I have taught you is the fruit, not of human study, but of prayer to the Mother of God. She first enlightened me with heavenly wisdom, and, lest I should be ensnared by pride, she warned me that shortly before my death my memory would suddenly fail. This has now happened; I know therefore that my end is at hand.' He closed his book, commended his soul to the prayers of his scholars, and cheerfully bade them farewell. From that moment he thought only of God and his soul, and three months after died a Saint in the simple faith of a child.

'But you have the unction from the Holy One, and know all things.'—1 John ii. 20.

Twenty-sixth Day.
Resurrection.

EARLY on the first day of the week the holy women repaired to the sepulchre to embalm the Body of Jesus. Mary alone remained at home, never doubting that He would rise, as He said, on the third day. The last sight of Jesus, stiff in death, had possessed her soul during that second weary night, when suddenly the room trembled, and amidst floods of light her risen Lord stood forth. Was ever joy like Mary's, as, prostrate in adoration, she gazed on the awful beauty of Body, Soul, and Godhead now again united, and heard once more the voice of her Son in holy converse with her? That bright and glorious Flesh had been taken from her substance, nourished with her life, tended by her in infancy, and swathed in death. 'He had risen, as He said,' and the fulfilment of His promise was the triumph of her faith. He had preached the Cross as the way to heaven, the dying to rise again; 'Mary had heard the word, and kept it,' and now His truth is manifest and His word confirmed. In the dark hour of His Passion, when others fled, Mary never ceased to worship Him as God; and now His divinity is proclaimed. Saints and Apostles are about to adore Him as their Sovereign Lord. But Mary, the foremost in sharing His sorrow and shame, was the first partaker of the joy of Jesus risen, and held the first place of honour in His triumph.—*Causa nostræ lætitiæ, ora pro nobis.*

Joy in Christ's Service.

Ours is the service of Jesus risen. He has borne our sorrows, and washed away our sins. Therefore His yoke is sweet and full of peace and joy.

'May the soul of Mary be in each, to magnify the Lord! May the spirit of Mary be in each, to rejoice in God!'—*S. Ambrose.*

S. Teresa, a motherless child of twelve years, put herself under the protection of Mary, and was shown afterwards in a vision that, but for the prayers of our Lady and S. Joseph, she would have been with the lost in hell. Among other favours granted to her was a vision of the risen Jesus. First the Hands, then the whole Figure, and the Sacred Face itself, in all its indescribable beauty, were revealed to the Saint. The lustre of the Divine Presence was such that the noonday sun seemed but a cloud in comparison, and its light withal was so soft and delicate, that the soul never wearied of gazing upon it. 'No one,' she said, 'who had ever seen this sight could wish to open his eyes again.' Her own soul was set on fire by the vision, and became so completely detached from things of earth, that at the moment of death it darted like a brilliant flame to heaven.

'You shall draw waters with joy out of the Saviour's fountains.'—Isai. xii. 3.

Twenty-seventh Day.
Ascension.

AFTER the Resurrection our Blessed Lord appeared to His disciples from time to time, but His home during the forty days was once more with His Mother at Nazareth. There, for long years, He had trained her as the Mother of His elect, and He would devote His last days on earth to fitting her for her mighty office. She was nearest to Him when He led His disciples out to Olivet, and on Mary descended, in all its fulness, His final benediction. Her eyes followed Him as He rose by His own might, with attendant Angels and the Saints delivered from Limbus, and her soul was filled with exceeding joy as the clouds hid Him from sight. Yet Jesus was then more distant from her than when His Body lay buried in the tomb,—how could she rejoice? Free from all thought of self, Mary had but two loves—Jesus and ourselves, or rather, ourselves in Him. With the eye of faith she beheld her Son at His Father's right hand, and dearer than His presence was His glory to her. In ourselves she saw Him, and had a mother's work to do. Jesus, though ascended on high, impassible and glorious, was still on earth, suffering and weak as in His earliest days. His mystical Body was scarcely formed; in Mary's arms its safety lay. With joy, therefore, she remained on earth, as Jesus had instructed her, to nourish with divine milk the infant Church, and to be its guide to heaven.—*Janua cœli, ora pro nobis.*

Unselfish Aims.

Seek your reward not here but hereafter, and spend yourself for your neighbour, that in death you may find yourself with God.

'Aim at this, pray for this, desire this, that thou mayest be divested of all self-seeking: and thus naked, follow Jesus naked, and eternally live with Me.'—*Imitation.*

S. Charles Borromeo, at the age of twenty-two, was Archbishop of Milan and Cardinal of Holy Church, with most brilliant prospects before him. But his only desire was to labour for souls. He toiled among the poor and sick more unweariedly than the humblest priest. His guide in this life of detachment was our Lady. He said her Office and Rosary daily on his knees; he fasted on her vigils; and at the sound of the *Angelus* he would dismount from his horse and kneel in the muddy road, to recite it with due reverence. He instituted processions in honour of Mary on the first Sunday of the month, and instructed his flock to bow the head at mention of her sweet name. On Saturdays a bell rang in every parish to summon the people to church to sing our Lady's Antiphon, and over the porch by which they entered was hung a picture of her, whom S. Charles reverenced as truly the gate of heaven.

'Charity seeketh not her own.'—1 Cor. xiii. 5.

Twenty-eighth Day.
Pentecost.

ACCORDING to our Lord's command, our Blessed Lady returned from Mount Olivet to Jerusalem, and gathered the Apostles round her in the cœnaculum. There, hidden from the sight or sound of men, she taught them to detach themselves from earthly things, and, by united prayer and repeated acts of desire, to hasten the Spirit's descent. It was the first Novena of the Church on earth. Saints and penitents, rulers and subjects, were gathered in that one room, whose narrow precincts held the best that earth had of faith, hope, and charity. At length, on the tenth day, the answer came, suddenly, as a mighty rushing wind. One moment the Spirit hung over the head of Mary, His Spouse, then broke upon the heads of all present in cloven tongues of fire. Twice already—at her Conception and at the Annunciation—the Holy Ghost had descended on Mary's soul; but this third sanctification was for ourselves as well. At Pentecost the living Church was perfected in truth and grace, and Mary offered to her Son the first-fruits of His harvest. The Apostles were transformed. They went forth new men, to preach and suffer with that burning faith and zeal which ever mark the rulers of God's Church. So always the Spirit descends through Mary's hands, and in answer to her prayer, begetting of her the members of Christ's Body, as of her He had first begotten the Head.—*Regina Apostolorum, ora pro nobis.*

Devotion to the Holy Ghost.

The Holy Spirit is the gift of God, but He is also the Spouse of Mary. Ask her that He may ever dwell within you.

'O Mary, that grace of the Holy Spirit, which others have in part, thou alone possessest wholly.' —*S. Bernard.*

When S. Gregory Thaumaturgus was made bishop, the thought of his responsibilities filled him with fear, and he obtained leave to retire again for a while to seek light of the Holy Spirit. One night, as he lay awake in his cell, pondering on the mysteries of the faith, an old man entered and pointed to a Lady radiant with heavenly beauty. This old man was S. John the Evangelist; and when the Lady bade S. John explain to him the sacred truths, S. John replied that he would indeed do whatever was pleasing to the Mother of his Lord. Then he set before Gregory the whole Christian Creed, which the bishop put into writing. He started for his see, the heathen city of Neocæsarea, without money or friends, but he trusted to Mary; and in answer to her prayers the Spirit of God so strengthened his work, that when he came to die in the same city, where he had found but seventeen Christians, only seventeen heathens were left.

'All thy children shall be taught of the Lord, and great shall be the peace of thy children.'— Isai. liv. 13.

Twenty-ninth Day.
Death.

FOR fifteen years after the Ascension our Blessed Lady remained on earth. The first Christians flocked to her from all sides. Her words enlightened their faith; her example gave them courage; the very sight of her enkindled the love of God. Frequently she visited Calvary and other places made holy by the footsteps of Christ. Daily she received the Holy Eucharist from the hands of S. John. At length, in her sixty-fourth year, the term of her exile approached, for her work in the Church was done, and the sum of her merits was complete. An angel warned her of her coming release, for there was no sign of weakness to foretell its approach. The grace which exempted her from Adam's sin had purified her flesh from defilement, and prevented all decay. The power of her mighty soul was unimpaired; every faculty, sense, and organ was acting with vigorous life. Yet she was to die, not for herself, or because of sin, but to fulfil a condition of our nature, to be in dying one with us, and to do as Jesus did. By divine power the Apostles were transported to her presence from the various parts of the world, and knelt for their Mother's blessing for the last time on earth.

Then, with no strife of flesh or spirit, but solely from the force of divine love, Mary died, and her soul broke from its earthly tenement to take possession of heaven.—*Virgo fidelis, ora pro nobis.*

Conformity to the Will of God.

Endeavour to be ready to work or rest, to live or die, only as God wishes.

'I wish, from the bottom of my heart, to be fortified by the Sacraments before I die; but I have the hardihood to prefer the providence of my Lord and my God to all the Sacraments; and I think this the safest preparation for death.'—*S. Gertrude.*

S. Gertrude was instructed by our Lord Himself how to honour His Mother, and Mary in return fastened on her heart a heavenly jewel which mystically expressed the virtues most dear to Jesus. The will of God impressed itself upon the soul of Gertrude as upon wax softened by fire; and at times she became conscious of all the pulsations of the Heart of Jesus, and understood their meaning. His will was to her all in all. She would take of her own choice nothing, however trifling, but stretched out her hand with her eyes closed, that she might receive all as a gift from God. A long and most painful illness tested her patience, till Mary obtained for her as a last favour to die, as she herself had died, from the force of divine love, and to breathe forth her soul with great joy into the safe and eternal sanctuary of the Sacred Heart of Jesus.

'My meat is to do the will of Him that sent Me, that I may perfect His work.'—John iv. 34.

Thirtieth Day.
Assumption.

UNDER the olive-trees and amidst the flowers of Gethsemani, where Jesus had knelt in agony, the body of Mary was laid. Though the last rites were finished, the Apostles still lingered round the grave, for day and night angelic choirs were heard singing with glad voices the praises of their Queen. On the third day the music ceased, and the Apostles were preparing to depart, when S. Thomas arrived amongst them, and begged to adore the sacred relics. He was led to the tomb. It was open, and, instead of the pure and fragrant body, flowers were growing from the earth which the flesh of Mary had touched. Thus was announced the glorious truth. Death and corruption had no part in her. She had died because Jesus had died; her body, like His, had been laid in the tomb, that on the third day she too might rise again. The triumph of Jesus would indeed have been incomplete if its noblest trophy, the one creature perfectly redeemed, lay mouldering in the grave. His Sacred Heart yearned for the bodily presence of the Mother who had ministered to Him in life and death. Mary herself longed more than patriarch or saint that in her flesh she might see God, and be finally perfected in Him. Therefore on the third day her desire was granted. She assumed her immaculate body, and soared aloft on the wings of the angels to the right hand of God.—*Regina angelorum, ora pro nobis.*

Frequent Thought of Heaven.

Heaven turns death to life. The thought of it changes sorrow to joy, and should be often in your heart.

'Let us take wing and fly on high, dear brethren. Let us go to eternal life.'—*S. John of the Cross.*

S. John of the Cross, the sage and seer of Carmel, was twice saved in his childhood from drowning by a Lady of heavenly beauty, whom none but himself saw. This vision of Mary never faded from his mind, and in his greatest suffering our Lady appeared, like a star piercing the darkness, to point to his eternal home. When he lay in prison, forgotten as one dead, the soft light of Mary's presence streamed forth in his dungeon and aided him to escape. Mary again led him through 'the obscure night' of darkness and desolation, and taught him how to kindle in his soul 'the flame of divine love' by the thought of the vision of God. The beauty of this thought made him long for death as others do for life. At length his desire was granted. On Saturday within the Octave of Mary's Immaculate Conception he went, as he said, full of joy to sing her Matins in heaven.

'Look up to heaven and see, and behold the sky that it is higher than thee.'—Job xxxv. 5.

Thirty-first Day.
Coronation.

ETERNAL shame fell upon Lucifer and the rebel spirits who refused honour to Mary and her Son, and it is the glory of the holy angels that they worshipped in their hour of trial the humble Virgin Mother. With great joy, therefore, did each order of the glorious spirits offer to the risen Mary their homage and obedience as she passed through their choirs to the right hand of Jesus, there to be crowned by the Holy Trinity, Queen of Angels and Saints, mediatrix of fallen man, the appointed channel of every grace. The privileges and crowns of each Saint are eminently hers; and nearest to the throne, she beholds the face of God more clearly than them all. Clothed with the sun, crowned with twelve stars, and with the moon beneath her feet, she holds the dominion of mercy over heaven and earth. God's will and hers are one, and her supplications are never unheard; her voice leads the worship of the blest, and through Mary the prayer of the Church rises like a sweet incense in the sight of the Most High. Her hands dispense every grace which descends on man, for by her Jesus began and consummated the redemption of the world. Seated on her throne, by the side of Christ her Son, and surrounded by the twelve Apostles, Mary reigns now and ever the Mother of the predestinate, our guiding light to heaven, and when we enter there, she is part of our heaven itself.—*Regina Sanctorum omnium, ora pro nobis.*

Love of the Church.

Every soul saved in the one true Church is a fresh jewel in Mary's crown. Love, then, our Holy Mother the Church. She alone gathers in the elect and increases the glory of Mary.

'Let us love God as our Father and the Church as our Mother.'—*S. Augustine.*

When S. Thomas of Canterbury was an infant his mother used to place him in a scale, and give to the poor in honour of our Blessed Lady an alms of food and clothes equal to his weight. Mary in return became the guide and patroness of his life. As he lay on a sick-bed she stood before him in her beauty as the Queen of Paradise, promised him health, and gave the keys of heaven to his charge. He wore a hair-shirt night and day in Mary's honour, and during the trials and sorrows of his episcopate he refreshed his spirit by repeating daily seven Aves in honour of her seven earthly joys. Once when he thus prayed, Mary appeared and bade him thank God also for the seven joys which are hers for eternity; and promised that all who do this should be blessed by her presence in death, and share with her the joys of Paradise. So it proved with S. Thomas. As the assassins fell upon him he recommended his soul to Mary's care, and thus won the grace of perseverance and the martyr's crown.

'This is the way; walk ye in it.'—Isai. xxx. 21.

www.ingramcontent.com/pod-product-compliance
Lightning Source LLC
Chambersburg PA
CBHW020246090426
42735CB00010B/1860